How to Teach Your Children Manners

HOW TO TEACH YOUR CHILDREN MANNERS

Essential Life Skills Your Child Needs to Know!

By Rebecca Black

CELESTIAL ARC PUBLISHING

Copyright © 2002 Rebecca Black. All rights reserved. This book is not to be reproduced or shared without permission from Rebecca Black.

Revised and Rewritten. Second Edition 2019

CELESTIAL ARC PUBLISHING

ISBN-13: 978-1544679990
ISBN-10: 1544679998

DEDICATION

To my dearest friend and loving husband Walker Black. You have been my most ardent supporter and the very best editor a writer can have.

CONTENTS

Introduction 13
Chapter One: Teaching Respect & Consideration 15
    How To Teach The Basics 16
        The Teachable Moment... 16
    Creating a Loving Home... 18
    Share Private Time to Teach Values 20
    Chores are More Than Taking Out the Trash............................ 21
    Sharing Common Rooms 22
    Guests Manners.. 23
    Behaviors to Teach 25
Chapter Two: Communication Skills 27
    Non-Verbal Communication 28
        Teaching Self-Confidence 28
        Appearances 30
        Proper Hygiene 30
        Attire.. 31
    Verbal Communication... 32
        Proper Introductions and Greetings..................................... 32
        Rules of Introductions 32
        Starting a Conversation... 33
        Teach Your Child to Self-Correct 34
        Quiet... 34

Telephone Etiquette 35
Electronic Communication 37
    CellPhone Text Messaging 37
    Email and Instant Messaging 38
    Cellphone Etiquette 39
    Social Networking 40
Written Communication 41
    Envelope 42
    The Correct Forms of Address 42
    Letters to Government Officials 43
    Formal Invitations 44
    Informal Invitation 45
    Thank You Note 45
    Condolence Note 46

Chapter Three: Behavior in Shared Spaces 47
Modeling Respectful & Considerate Behavior 48
    Attend to Attire 49
    Expected Behavior 50
Dining Out 54
Graduation 55
    Note 55
Popularity vs Friendship 56

Chapter Four: Teaching Problem Solving 57
Fine Tune Your Calm 58

Chapter Five: Safety vs. Manners 61
    Strangers May be Strange 62
    Safety Messures 64
        When Your Child is Away From Home 64
        When He/She is at Home 64

Chapter Six: Teaching Table Manners 67
    The Importance of Table Manners 68
    It May Be Challenging! 70
    How Are Your Table Manners? 71
    A Bit of History 72
    Table Behavior 74
        Which Utensil? 75
        Wait Until All Are Served 75
        About Your Napkin 76
        Napkin Rules 77
        Strange Foods 77
        Obscure Rules 77
        Sensitive Issues 78
        Elbows In! 79
        Mother Recommended Rules 80
        Bread and Butter Rules 80
        Do Not 81
    Setting the Table 83
    Holding and Using Utensils 85

The American Method 86
    American Method Trivia 86
    How to Use the American Method 87
The Continental Method 88
    How to Use the Continental Method 88
Eating Soup 89
    Basic Tips 89
Body Language & Table Conversation 90
    Body Language 90
    Rules to Remember 91
    Table Conversation 92
Styles of Meals 93
    Formality Matters 93
    Family Style Meals 94
    Formal Meals 94
    Formal Meal Rules 95
Behaviors to Teach 96

Chapter Seven: Dining Out 97
The Importance of Table Manners While Dining Out 98
Dining Out Basics 101
Gentle Reminders 102

Chapter Eight: Fingers, Fork and Knife 103
I Really Need to Know This! 104
Common Finger Foods 105

How Do I Eat These? 107
Chapter Nine: The Workbook **115**
Let's Review 116
Your Author **125**

INTRODUCTION

"Son, always tell the truth. Then you'll never have to remember what you said the last time." Sam Rayburn

I would like to share a true story about how I decided to teach and then write about this subject. While dining out one evening, my husband and I witnessed a young boy, approximately ten, playing soccer with a straw inside the restaurant, while his father was sitting only a few feet away from him. No kidding.

It seemed as if he was trying to see how high he could kick it. I could almost hear the cheers of the crowd. While Father saw what Mr. Soccer was doing, there was no indication that he found fault in his son's actions, as he did nothing. I thought, "What a terrible loss of a teachable moment". Dad should have known that a restaurant is no place for a soccer game and taught his son as much.

We will begin to learn how to teach our children manners by learning to recognize what a "teachable moment" is. Please read on.

CHAPTER ONE
TEACHING RESPECT & CONSIDERATION

HOW TO TEACH THE BASICS

Unfortunately, many parents miss crucial teachable moments. To prevent this happening to you, allow me to describe what a teachable moment is.

THE TEACHABLE MOMENT

Imagine that you are walking with your child and he steps off the sidewalk into someone's flowerbed; *this is a teachable moment.* At this moment, as your child's *manners* teacher you would tell him to "Stop." "Look down at your feet." "Where are they?" "Where should they be?" "What should you do now?" Your reaction teaches your child respect, consideration, and responsibility.

Unfortunately, I too have missed teachable moments in my children's childhood. When my daughter was a teen, she was a member of the high school basketball team. During one of her games, she fouled out within the first half hour. Honestly, she looked as if she was playing pro-hockey; girls from the other team were flying into the walls. We discussed her behavior after the game, but I should have talked to her immediately. When you witness aggression, pounce on the opportunity for open dialogue. Problem solving and anger control begins at a *young* age and is derived from you.

There is no better place to begin our journey to better manners than in our own home. How do you treat your significant other? With respect and love, I hope. When your child witnesses your kindness and thoughtfulness, she will use the same behavior. Talk to your child and include her in discussions, never belittling her or others in her presence. Such behavior causes deep pain and anger.

Children learn how to treat others from your example.

Consequently, you see that you are the teacher here. Your child will have no better teacher in his life. Model exemplary behavior and live it; it becomes a part of you and a part of your child. As your child witnesses this, he will learn to *value* others.

CREATING A LOVING HOME

My husband and I don't have anyone to model loving behavior to, except our cat and she ignores us. However, he is always considerate of my needs.

For example, because he rises before me, he brings in the newspaper, so I won't have to walk to the driveway to retrieve it. In addition, if the water container is almost empty, he puts a full container in the refrigerator for me. Conversely, I bake his favorite scones and open his favorite wine before he gets home. We love each other and show it every day in so many small ways.

Today's family is not an "Ozzie and Harriet" clone. Single parent, same-gender, or unmarried couples are quite common and are completely capable of creating happy, loving homes for their children. Whatever your family composition, you have the power to create that home; just remember that love and consideration come first.

Additionally, please remember that love and family include the extended family. Many of us may be called upon to assist family members in time of need. Our brothers, sisters, parents or even cousins may lose jobs or spouses and require time to regroup. This is an ideal time to teach your children the lesson of giving.

How do you demonstrate to your family that you care and *respect* them? This doesn't have to be a grand gesture, as each of us is eager to love. Begin with simple behaviors and gestures.

Listening is a wonderful beginning. Hugging them is another. Take the time, slow down and really listen to your child's stories and reward yourself with the best-ever hug. Better yet, sharing dinner and discussing the day is an excellent way to strengthen connections.

SHARE PRIVATE TIME TO TEACH VALUES

When my children were younger, we cooked together. It was a great collaboration; I love to cook, and they loved to eat.

My daughter just *had* to have wontons; which if you've ever made these you know it takes some time to make. She would sit with me and help wrap. We would have this big bowl of filling between us and as we wrapped, we *talked*. It was a perfect way to find out who she was at that time in her life and for her to learn my values. She was a captive audience—not unlike children during bedtime.

Dinner and bedtime offer many teachable moments.

When you put your children to bed, do you take the time for stories? I know we are all very busy these days, but this is a *significant* teachable moment. There are great stories that teach respect, love, and taking responsibility. Please, don't miss this opportunity.

CHORES ARE MORE THAN TAKING OUT THE TRASH

Many of us are fortunate to live in comfortable, pleasant homes with an abundance of excellent food available to us. Of course, our children share in this great bounty. Yet, are our children helping in the upkeep or sharing in the daily duties?

All children wish to feel valued, needed, and wanted. Chores offer them a feeling of responsibility and children begin to feel as if they are part of a unit. They will also learn that we all work together. Through these activities, responsibility, respect for others, and respect for property are learned.

SHARING COMMON ROOMS

Care and use of common rooms help teach responsibility. If we allow our children to leave items in our living areas, such as empty soda cans, glasses and toys, they may conclude that this is normal. Perhaps they may also conclude that a *cleaning fairy* cleans while they are sleeping.

  Thus, we should teach our children to leave each room the way they found it or better by cleaning and putting items away. When age appropriate, they should learn to do their own dishes, take care of their wet towels, clean the tub and wipe down the shower and to always replace toilet paper when roll is empty.

  As your child ages, he/she should also do laundry. Therefore, teach this as a life skill along with cleaning messes in the microwave and refrigerator, and rinsing dishes before loading them into the dishwasher.

GUESTS MANNERS

When your child has guests, it is best that they properly introduce them to you. Younger people are always introduced to older. Consequently, he/she would introduce your friend to you. For example, "Mother, I would like to introduce to you, my friend from school, Juan Gutierrez." "Juan, this is my mother, Mrs. James."

They should treat their friends as special. This means that he/she would give guests the best chair, let them choose the first movie or game, and allow them to make the decision between pizza and hot dogs. It's imperative that they inform guests which rooms are off limits and other rules of the home. They wouldn't want their friends to be embarrassed by waking family members who work nights.

When you have guests, they should be on their best behavior. This is a time to show off their impeccable manners.

If he/she is sitting when the guest arrives, he/she should greet that person properly. This is great practice for those times that he/she may meet representatives from companies at career fairs in their future.

He/she should turn the television or game down or off, stand, shake hands when that person extends hers/his, and say that it is nice to meet her/him.

BEHAVIORS TO TEACH

- We do not walk between people who are talking; if it is unavoidable, we say, "Excuse me."
- We do not yell in public places.
- We say please and thank you.
- We don't always have to be first.
- When someone is mean to us, we don't have to be mean in return.
- Teach proper introductions, greetings, and to write thank you notes.
- Email writing is an excellent way to practice our letter writing skills (use good grammar).

Moreover, remember, you are the role model, use good manners and your children will too.

CHAPTER TWO
COMMUNICATION SKILLS

NON-VERBAL COMMUNICATION

We begin our discussion of communication skills with non-verbal communication, which is basically body language. Typically, our children don't have an idea of body image. As you children become teens, they may focus on building muscles or dieting to slim down. However, most do not realize what their body language is saying to others.

Posture speaks volumes about how we feel about ourselves and our surroundings. Please try to help them realize how others might perceive them if they slouch or slump. When they stoop, with heads down making no eye contact, others will view them as insecure. Yet, if they walk tall with their heads up making good eye contact, others will view them as self-assured.

Aristotle stated, "People are virtuous because they act rightly." ...which means, that we do the right thing and then we become that virtuous person. How right he was. It is now widely known that our actions precede how we view ourselves. This is because others react to our behavior and actions.

TEACHING SELF-CONFIDENCE

Once upon a time not too long ago, a college professor asked his students to participate in a research study as part of their grade. He separated his students into groups and asked his students of psychology to pretend for a period-of-time to be popular, to be unpopular, and to be the average Joe or Jane.

At the end of the time-period, those who pretended to be popular were; those who pretended to be unpopular were, and those who pretended to be the average Joes/Janes were. What does this study illustrate? This tells us that people believe what they see. If we behave in a certain way, those around us believe it.

Actions precede feelings. In fact, many psychologists now concur. Therefore, if we pretend that we are self-confident and suave, others will notice, believe, and treat us as if we are; we mentally absorb this and become the person others believe we are. We will then become that person.

Also important is how we sit. When wearing slacks, females may cross one knee over another. Young men may also cross their legs. With skirts, females should cross their ankles because skirts ride up and may become too short. However, no one should sit with legs open! This appears as if the person has been riding a horse for a month!

Note

Please teach your child not to smack gum! It is noisy and very unattractive.

APPEARANCES

We have less than thirty seconds to make the first impression. Yes, it is true. Others judge us by our appearance in just a few seconds. Consequently, please help your child to look in the mirror and ask him/herself, "What impression am I making?"

PROPER HYGIENE

Have you had to sit next to someone with questionable hygiene? Not very pleasant, is it? It is important to teach our children that proper hygiene is crucial. Someone who is smelly is not someone we tend to gravitate toward, so it is best to help our children consider hygiene, as it is best not to be that smelly person. Therefore, teach him/her to bathe daily, which also includes brushing teeth, and washing hair.

In fact, proper hygiene is so important, one city created a hygiene mandate. A city official in a certain U.S. city states that one smelly employee is responsible for a new policy that requires all city employees to smell nice when at work. The policy reads that no employee shall have an odor generally offensive to others when reporting to work. An offensive body odor may result from a lack of good hygiene, from an excessive application of a fragrant aftershave or cologne or from another cause.

No, this is no joke, as exposure to a person who smells is no joke. Help your child avoid being that smelly person.

ATTIRE

As mentioned in the first chapter, attire choices are important. Our children learn from us every day about how our attire choices reflect who we are and how we view our environment.

For those special occasions, they should avoid stomach revealing, tight fitting tops, short skirts, shorts, pants that hang around the lower hips and flip-flops.

Note

Please no hats indoors! This includes baseball hats.

VERBAL COMMUNICATION

Communication is imperative in all our relationships. Can you imagine a good relationship with your significant other without good communication? It wouldn't last long. Nevertheless, let's consider the most important component of communication. If you guessed listening, you are correct. We need to listen to everyone when he or she speaks. Therefore, we need to teach our children to listen attentively.

PROPER INTRODUCTIONS AND GREETINGS

We cannot begin a relationship without being introduced. Introductions and greetings are essential.

If your child is introducing him/herself, he/she needs to stand, extend his/her hand and say, "Hello my name is first and last name" and when the person says his or her name he/she should repeat it and say that it is nice to meet her/him. This will help your child remember her name.

Please introduce others by mentioning first and last names with a bit of information about them.

RULES OF INTRODUCTIONS

There is a hierarchy for introducing one to another. Younger people are introduced to their elders: Mom, "This is my college roommate Juan Gutierrez." Juan, "This is my mother,

Jacklyn Crowder." Introduce guests to hosts. Additionally, as a sign of respect, introduce people to others with higher standings such as senator, governor, mayor, clergy, etc. Finally, it is best if your child avoids introducing anyone as his/her friend because that implies the other person may not be his/her friend.

STARTING A CONVERSATION

Teaching our children how to become a good conversationalist is not impossible; it just requires practice. We may start with the information given to us. Asking how the person knows a common friend is a good start, as well as making comments such as, "Tell me about yourself."

Other great conversation starters are listening to what he or she says and follow up with the theme. So, if this person is talking about golf, ask specific questions about golf and golfing. Mentioning music that may be playing in the background. Inquire about that person's preferences.

Of course, we would want to avoid ethnic jokes, slurs, politics, and religion. These topics can create a negative atmosphere. Also, we must avoid gossip. Gossip is a destructive force that can ruin relationships. Please help your child realize that if he/she were to gossip about someone, the person hearing it may wonder what he/she say behind his or her back.

One precaution to teach is that we shouldn't reveal too much personal information in the beginning of our relationships. Your child might have the neighborhood gossip telling everyone how he/she sings to his/her cat every morning.

TEACH YOUR CHILD TO SELF-CORRECT

Part of being a parent is helping our children to become aware of his and her behaviors. Observe your child for whining, using the same words repeatedly, cussing and grunting. All these noises will define your child to others. Listen carefully to all of the noises your child makes and help him or her adjust the volume.

QUIET

Quiet is expected in most public places, such as waiting rooms, busses and libraries. Why is this so? Well, in most of these places we wish to think and reflect in quiet. Thus, if we make noise by talking excessively or loudly, we affect others' personal space. We all have a space around us that includes a quiet quotient. We should respect this.

TELEPHONE ETIQUETTE

Many do not use a landline telephone anymore. For those who do, the following information is for you. Please help your child to be mindful of the length of his/her calls if the family shares a landline phone. Your child should identify him/herself when making a call. Therefore, if your child calls a friend named Joe, he could say, "Hello, my name is John Abernathy, calling for Joe. May I speak to him please?"

However, as I mention in more detail later in this book, your child should not identify him or herself when receiving a call. We need to consider our safety first. A proper response when someone asks for your child's name could be, "With whom do you wish to speak?"

Additionally, your child should not call someone too often or before 8 am or after 9 pm.

It is perfectly appropriate for young ladies to call young men these days; it is no longer considered improper. In addition, he/she should always ask if this is a good time to talk.

If your child dials a wrong number, he/she should apologize and check the number called.

Please teach your child to always sound interested in what the caller is talking about and do not do anything else while the caller is talking. Often my sister will be doing the dishes or some other chore while we are talking. I'm left wondering if she is listening to me at all.

Moreover, he/she should excuse him or herself to the caller when talking to someone else in the room. It is irritating to the caller to wonder to whom your child is talking.

Instruct your child not to eat while on the phone. Your caller should feel as if he or she is important.

When taking messages, your child should ask for the caller's first and last name, plus the proper spelling. Ask for the caller's phone number; ask when the call may be returned and the purpose of the call.

ELECTRONIC COMMUNICATION

Today, electronic communication is pervasive. For many, text messaging has surpassed the popularity of email because it is fun, quick, and effective. Nevertheless, we need to observe some etiquette. We would not want to be rude to those with whom we communicate. What follows is what we should be teaching.

CELLPHONE TEXT MESSAGING

Do not text someone, while in the company of another.

- It is considered as rude as taking a voice call.

Text messaging is informal.

- Do not use it for formal invitations.

Do not dissolve a relationship using text messaging.

Be patient while waiting for a reply.

- Watch your frustration level.
- Your recipient may not be as adept at texting as you.

Be aware of your tone.

- Your message can be misinterpreted entirely. Reread your messages carefully.

Texting while driving is dangerous.

- There is no possible way anyone can watch the road and text at the same time.

Watch your slang.
- Yes, this is an informal form of communication, but the slang can become part of your everyday language.
- Stay on top of your game with proper grammar.

Texting can be traced.
- Do not send messages that may be perceived as improper.

EMAIL AND INSTANT MESSAGING

Please teach your children to respond to email as quickly as possible using good judgment in language. Additionally, anyone can see an email; it is not private. Therefore, none of us would not want to write anything that we wouldn't want posted on a bulletin board.

Email is a form of writing, so we always use good grammar, spelling, and tone.

Instant messaging is now back in vogue and can be an enjoyable activity; but is not private and sometimes is not safe, especially in the social networking world. Please teach your children to be careful.

If your children are old enough to Tweet or message someone on social networking sites – such as Facebook – suggest to your child to always ask the recipient if he/she has the time to converse. I have friends who continually want to engage in a lengthy conversation on-line. My answer is always the same. I simply don't have time. Therefore, I appear off-line all day.

Additionally, it is considered impolite to invite someone to join an instant-messaging conversation that is ongoing without asking the others who are conversing first. The same goes for Google Hangouts.

CELLPHONE ETIQUETTE

Do

- Remove Blue Tooth device when with others.

No Ringing

- In a restaurant and in a theater during a movie
- During a doctor/dental exam.
- During an interview.
- At the golf course.
- During a discussion.
- In the library, a place of worship, in court, and in hospitals.

Avoid Conversing

- In every situation mentioned above.
- While a checker in a store is ringing up your purchases.
- During a haircut or styling.

Avoid loud melodic ringing in public places

SOCIAL NETWORKING

Number One Rule to Teach Children

On social networking sites, or any other, never write anything you wouldn't say to another person face to face.

Avoid

- Cyber dumping
- Sharing personal information
- Posting racy or potentially embarrassing photos
- Posting hateful or untruthful gossip about others
- Using profanities or poor grammar

WRITTEN COMMUNICATION

When is the last time your child sent a thank you card? ...a sympathy card? These niceties create lasting friendships and indicate to others that your child is a polite, caring and socially adept person.

There is no substitution for a handwritten card sent via snail mail when it comes to thank you or sympathy card. For birthday cards, email is considered passable, but is still not on par with the 'real' thing. Moreover, we would never use email for sympathy cards.

Choose nice stationary with playful colors for letters to family and friends. Choose neutral colors, gray, white, and cream for business letters. Use pen, not pencil, for a more formal appearance. Always, type your business letters.

ENVELOPE

Mr. James Wilson

223 Adams Street

Jackson, Mississippi 23343

                      Ms. Elizabeth Jones

                      588 Washington Road

                      Claremont, Louisiana 22398

THE CORRECT FORMS OF ADDRESS

Boys under 7

- Master John Smith
- Dear John

Boys 7-18

- John Smith
- Dear John

Man 18 or over

- Mr. John Smith
- Dear Mr. Smith or Dear John

Unmarried girl

- Miss/Ms. Jane Jones
- Dear Jane or Dear Miss/Ms. Jones

Woman
- Ms. Jane Jones
- Dear Ms. Jones

Married
- Mrs./Ms. Jane Jones
- Dear Mrs./Ms. Jones

Divorced
- Mrs./Ms. Jane Jones
- Dear Mrs./Ms. Jones

Widowed
- Mrs. John Jones
- Dear Mrs. Jones

LETTERS TO GOVERNMENT OFFICIALS

The Letter

123 Cherry Lane

Sonoma, California 94532

Date

Dear Senator Boxer:

Respectfully,

Me

The Envelope

Mr. First Last Name

Address

City, State Zip Code

> The Honorable Barbara Boxer
>
> 112 Hart Building
>
> Washington, DC 20510

FORMAL INVITATIONS

Mr. and Mrs. Juan Ortiz

request the pleasure of your company

on Sunday, the twentieth of June

at three o'clock

R.S.V.P.

35 Clark Place

Joy Land, Oregon

This should be mailed at least eight weeks in advance.

The Response

Ms. Rebecca Black

accepts with pleasure

Or

regrets that she is unable to accept

your kind invitation

for

Sunday, the twentieth of June

INFORMAL INVITATION

Birthday Party

Shannon Brown

Date

2 P.M. to 5 P.M.

THANK YOU NOTE

Date

Dear Aunt Jane,

    I love my new chessboard; thank you. I have already beaten my dad twice. Maybe we can play a game the next time you come to visit.

    See you soon.

Love,

Peggy

CONDOLENCE NOTE

Date

Dear Frank,

    I just learned of the death of your mother. I know how much she meant to you, so this must be very difficult for you. Please accept my deepest sympathies and know that I am always thinking of you. Please call if there is anything I can do.

Sincerely,

Jane Drummond

CHAPTER THREE
BEHAVIOR IN SHARED SPACES

MODELING RESPECTFUL & CONSIDERATE BEHAVIOR

Social events can be excellent teachable moments for teaching children to exhibit respect and consideration for others.

We demonstrate these qualities as we arrive for social events, medical appointments, school functions, and restaurant reservations *at* the appointed time. When we make others wait for us or behave in a disruptive manner in public, we are modeling dismissive behavior.

Some of us even use our cellphones during a live performance or in a fine dining establishment. Although we are all part of this bustling 21st century, we must weigh our consideration for those around us with our need to have constant access to the wired 24/7 world.

While purchasing coffee at our favorite shop recently, we became engaged in a long conversation with one of the owners. I was telling her about my manners classes and she just gushed forward with a long tirade about the families who frequent her store. She told us that one child (whose father was nearby) was jumping on one of her couches. She was afraid the child would fall and he was damaging the furniture. The father became quite angry with her when she asked the little boy to stop jumping.

This was a teachable moment, but I think the father needed more help than the child. The parent's behavior did nothing to teach the child to respect property or others. By the way, the owner called the room with the couches the living room. It is, indeed, *her* living room.

ATTEND TO ATTIRE

One of the things I love about these *modern* times we live in is that we are more relaxed about our dress. In the university town in which we live, people go to the coffee shop in their sweats and no one thinks anything about it. It is wonderful to feel so free. However, we should consider the level of casualness we have created. While it is appropriate to dress in t-shirts and jeans to go to the grocery store, it is not proper attire for the ballet. When we *dress-up* for an event, our child feels excited and stands just a bit taller. Insisting on wearing formal attire for formal events teaches him to have respect for himself and for those sponsoring the event.

"When in doubt, tell the truth." Mark Twain

EXPECTED BEHAVIOR

A certain type of behavior is expected in these public or shared spaces. We begin by teaching basic 'good manners' when we are in public; treating others as we wish to be treated.

Consequently, help our child avoid jumping to conclusions about others. That 'nerdish' looking guy in front of you in line just may be the next Bill Gates. This will also help our child avoid becoming a bully and to also recognize one.

Moreover, because people do jump to conclusions about others, we should always think about how our behavior may influence another's view of us before they even get to know us. This is an important lesson for all of us, especially our children.

Our behavior affects those around us. What we do in our space affects others. Therefore, we need to revisit our children's posture.

Why is it so important? As I mentioned before, your child's posture directly affects how others perceive him/her. Consequently, if he/she appears as a confident person, standing tall, looking forward, smiling, and making eye contact, others will believe that he/she is that confident person.

Please remind your child to always obey the rules posted at malls, parks, zoos, etc. This means no loitering, no skateboards, and no visiting parks after 10 pm. Hey, they shouldn't be out that late anyway.

There is an etiquette involved when it comes to elevators. If the elevator is crowded, the persons closest to the door exit first. Gender is not an issue in this case. However, if it is not crowded, women and girls enter and leave first. The one exception is if there are elderly onboard. Older people are considered most important—we give those much older than ourselves respect. The person closest to the "Door Open" button should hold it until everyone who wants out is out and those who want in are in.

We all know that we should hold the door for people, but for whom and when? We should hold the door for someone carrying packages, for a mother with a stroller and anyone needing assistance, such as someone in a wheelchair. Men should hold doors for women. It is a gentlemanly gesture. Finally, we should hold the door for anyone close behind us. Can you imagine watching our child allow a door to close in another's face? As good parents, we wouldn't want our child to face embarrassment like that.

Because we want our children to demonstrate respect for those around us we should help them consider a few rules.

Be on time for appointments.

When we are late for an appointment, it is as if we are saying that our time is more valuable than their time.

Settle in before a show begins.

We should be seated in our seats, coats removed, packages of snacks opened, and not be rustling around when the show begins. We don't want to disturb those around us by making any kind of noise.

Turn off electronic equipment, especially cellphones.

It is irritating to most others to have to listen to someone else's phone conversation. Plus, to hear a cellphone ring during a movie is very disturbing.

Quiet

Most people want quiet in shared spaces. People want to enjoy the space without someone else interrupting their peace with loud voices.

Stay in your space.

Imagine sitting in a restaurant with those little tables and benches along a wall. You are on the bench. You have very little space between you and the next person sitting in front of her table. Please teach your child to be very conscious of how he/she uses that space. Teach him/her to consider where his/her jacket, purse, and backpack is.

Watch temper and language.

There are times that your child might feel angry. Please help your child channel that anger in a positive direction. Teach that his/her anger is your child's and that no one can 'make' him/her angry. This helps your child learn how to control the anger and not allow it to control him/her.

DINING OUT

Our children wouldn't want to be embarrassed or embarrass those around them while dining in a restaurant. When we visit a restaurant, any type of restaurant, we are just visiting. We need to show respect for property, for other diners and for those who work there. Please read the "Dining Our Basis" tutorial in Chapter Seven.

GRADUATION

Graduation is an exciting time, so help your teen by ensuing he/she graduates. High school can be challenging with hormones pulling and tugging teens in all directions and the pressure that their future may depend upon passing tests with high scores. Thus, try to observe your child for these pressures.

As for graduation, if family members need to travel, inform them very early of your teens graduation date. Suggest to your child to spend special time, perhaps a lunch, with those who cannot attend.

If your teen wants a limo, suggest that he/she earns money throughout the year to pay for it. Also, suggest that he/she calls for rates from several sources and share with a few friends. This teaches your child responsibility.

Your teen is required to attend graduation rehearsals. This is a once in a lifetime event, so he/she should try to enjoy each component of the activity. Ensure that he/she dresses and act appropriately, which means that your teen should wear dressy clothing under the gown and should not 'moon' the principal.

Note

- Please ensure that your teen handwrites thank you notes for graduation gifts promptly!

POPULARITY VS FRIENDSHIP

Is it important to be popular? To some of us being popular is ultimately important. Nevertheless, what is important is how we feel about ourselves. This is something we should be teaching our child. As, others will view our child more positively if he/she feels confident. Also, being a good person and doing *good* for others is vital, because that is what matters the most.

Whether your child is popular or not, it is best if he/she is a good friend to others. To be a good friend your child must be trustworthy, avoid gossip, or betray a trust. Help your child to be the type of friend that everyone knows can keep a secret, to be loyal and to stand by his/her friend during difficult times. Mention that he/she needs to listen to the friend, to be involved in the friend's life, always remembering his/her birthday.

When we think of those around us as special, we will be special to them.

CHAPTER FOUR
TEACHING PROBLEM SOLVING

FINE TUNE YOUR CALM

Your child learns how to problem solve by watching and listening to you as you interact with your business associates, friends, family, those obnoxious people who pull in front of you on the freeway, and that person who tries to sneak in front of you when you've been standing in line an hour.

Naturally, this implies that you must model the behavior you wish for your child to exhibit. If your child hears you yelling (losing control) at people when you are angry, he will too. He will not learn self-control. Moreover, in today's ever shrinking and crowded world, we need that essential quality.

How do you deal with difficult people? Sometimes it is difficult indeed. I must share a story with you about a situation my husband and I recently experienced. A homeless man approached and requested food from us as we were standing in the produce section of a grocery store. As we mentally processed his request and what our actions should be, which included following him around so he could choose what he wants or just buying him some fruit, he became angry. Due to those few seconds we took to consider his request, he felt devalued. Yelling at us, he walked away. I was silent. I could not think of anything to say. Perhaps that was the best thing to do. I don't know. Perhaps you can find the best way to handle a similar situation.

When similar issues puzzled me as a child, my mother would always ask me how much I *wanted* to solve the problem. She said that if I wanted to solve a problem, I could.

In many cases, when we have problems with people, it's because we don't trust them with our feelings. Therefore, if we are upset, we need to say that we are, not yell it. State what the problem is and what we believe the solution could be. Perhaps we are more a part of the problem than we think we are. Yet, we will never arrive at this realization until we want to solve the problem.

Monitor your child's problem solving skills and analyze those skills objectively. Talk to your children. Help them understand that a hit for a hit, a yell for a yell is never acceptable behavior. We live in a world of increasing violence and through our children we can prevent at least a portion of it.

Invaluable tools to help your child learn to control their anger and to problem solve is to set limits, boundaries, and rules. Designate parameters they understand. When you state these rules in a loving manner, they will feel safe and loved. As they go out in the world, they will take these rules with them and will instinctively know right from wrong.

Remember, to watch for those teachable moments and that you are their best teacher. Model the appropriate behavior.

CHAPTER FIVE
SAFETY VS. MANNERS

STRANGERS MAY BE STRANGE

Proper etiquette would have us teach our children to greet strangers with kindness. It is an unfortunate, unpleasant fact that our children need to avoid strangers. Nevertheless, this doesn't imply rudeness.

Modeling proper greetings (good morning, how do you do, etc.) is a necessary skill and your child should know how and when to use them. An opportune time would be when they are in your company.

In addition, we all know that they should not go anywhere with an adult even if they know him/her, unless you have told your children to. This is not rude. This is a must. In fact, this is probably the most important skill you can teach your child—to tell someone they know that they already have a ride home. I realize that this is contrary to most writings you will find. However, I am a teacher, mother and grandmother, so I believe in safety first. This is the 21st

century with an increasing population of some good and some not so.

Proper etiquette would also have your child identify him or herself on the phone when he or she answers it. Not in my book. For safety sake, she should say hello and then ask for whom the caller requests. If the caller wishes to know if an adult is home, she should always take a message and say that you are busy, unless, of course, you are home. This is proper and safe.

When your child calls a friend, she should identify herself.

SAFETY MESSURES

WHEN YOUR CHILD IS AWAY FROM HOME

This information is especially important and pertinent for teens.

Make sure his/her cellphone is charged.

He/she just may need to call you in an emergency.

Does he/she have a house key?

He/she may not be the first out of the house that day, but may be the first to return. It is essential for him/her to have that key on hand.

Never ride with strangers.

This seems like a no-brainer. Nevertheless, as I have already mentioned, sometimes we don't take situations as seriously as we should. That person he or she just met through a friend is still a stranger.

WHEN HE/SHE IS AT HOME

Please teach:

Pick up the mail and newspaper.

If there are newspapers lying out front, it could appear as an invitation to a burglar—as if no one is home. Moreover, you don't want someone getting your mail and giving them access to your family's personal information.

Lock all the doors.

This is a very simple rule often over-looked, but is vitally important. Check your windows also.

Never open the door for someone you don't know.

If he/she doesn't know the person, he/she shouldn't open the door. Sometimes we think that we should open the door when someone knocks because it is the 'polite' thing to do. Safety matters more.

List important numbers as speed-dial on cellphones.

We never know when an emergency may occur. When that time arrives, he/she may be too nervous to remember phone numbers or proper contacts. So, he/she should keep these handy. Of course, we all know 911!

Don't go into the home if something looks suspicious.

Seems like another no-brainer, but often teens and older children assume that they can handle anything or think they are being silly when afraid. If he/she suspects anything is out of place, they shouldn't venture into the home. The police are there to help. They should call from a safe location and the police will ensure that the home is safe to enter.

Keep you informed of every time he/she leaves.

Even if your child is going next door, he/she should notify you to lessen your anxiety. I once had a student who was going to the store on her bike. Her parents were at work and she didn't tell them where she was going. She fell into a ditch, broke her leg and laid there for hours because no one knew where she was. You can imagine worried her parents were.

Never take new medication when you are not present.

Even over-the-counter drugs that seem safe may not be safe for your child. Take for example a story from my childhood. Around the age of 14 years old, I woke up one morning not feeling well. I was dizzy and nauseated, but still wanted to go to school. I couldn't ask my parents for help because both had already left for work.

I decided to search our medicine cabinet for something to make me feel better. After reading labels of all the bottles, I found one for motion sickness. The label stated that it helps eliminate nausea and dizziness associated with motion sickness—close enough for me. I took one pill and I'm off to school.

During first period class, I felt as if I was going to pass out. My teacher took me aside and through his questioning, we found that the pill made me sick. It turned out that I am hypoglycemic. Silly me; I just needed food.

CHAPTER SIX
TEACHING TABLE MANNERS

THE IMPORTANCE OF TABLE MANNERS

"Animals feed, men eat, but only wise men know the art of dining" French Gastronome, Anthelme Brillat-Savarin

Why is it that we think of table manners when someone mentions etiquette? Perhaps it is because all manners derive from our need for civility and harmony. For that reason, we treat people kindly with consideration and respect.

Add it all up and it makes the dinner table is the best place to teach nearly all manners. This is because we use *all* of our manners at the table. We also *share* at the table and we want everyone to feel comfortable. If we concentrate on other's comfort level, our mistakes will be small.

If consideration and respect are the most important things to remember at the table, is it necessary to study table manners? Of course, we should. Since we want everyone to feel comfortable, our table manners rules and behaviors offer us order—a standard. The added benefit is that your child will feel more confident eating in public when he is proficient.

Give your children all the tools they need to succeed in the world.

Another story comes to mind. My husband and I were fortunate to have cruised recently and met many wonderful people. One of them was Frank whose company we enjoyed very much.

However, we only had one meal together and it was very *uncomfortable*.

Although I am not prudish or judgmental about another's table manners, I could not watch him eat. Hunched over his plate, he shoveled food into his mouth, holding his fork as a shovel, all the while carrying on a conversation. These infractions of table manners rules are the memories that flash into my mind as I think of Frank. It is unfortunate.

Most table manners are common sense.

Please don't allow bad table manners be the first thing people reflect upon when they think of your child.

IT MAY BE CHALLENGING!

Many families responded to a survey asking what one activity promoted positive family values. Overwhelmingly, the respondents chose the family dinner. In addition, the survey noted that the family dinner hour had shrunk to less than thirty minutes and the families met at that meal on the average of three times a week. That means that we have less than 1 ½ hours to share with our family at the table. So, we must squeeze as much as we can into that time.

HOW ARE YOUR TABLE MANNERS?

In order to begin teaching your children table manners, you may need a refresher.

What worries you about your table manners skills? Most likely, you are worried about picking up the wrong fork at a formal meal.

Not to worry, none of us uses five forks at a meal any more, and why should we. Our tables are rarely set with a full set of flatware and to be honest, let's reflect on the most important rule for the table: Everyone should feel comfortable at the table, so we don't do anything that would make them feel uncomfortable.

Even though we follow this one "main rule," we need to review some table manners' guidelines.

Before we begin, though, it is best to learn a bit of history and trivia, so we have a good appreciation of what table manners are and how it has evolved.

A BIT OF HISTORY

History tells us that the first modern eating utensil was the knife. During early Roman times, we all carried our eating utensil with us; these were used more as a stabbing and slicing utensil and were even buried with us.

As time marched on, knives remained a popular eating utensil. We even find that knives were used at the table in 5th century, Saxon England. It appeared that men always carried one for their own use and also to cut meat for women.

How about the rounded edge knife? In France, many years ago, 1669 to be exact, there was a King Louis. This particular King, King Louis XIV, decided that to have weapons at the table was not a great idea. Therefore, he created a law stating that all table knives were to be rounded. Actually, this is why, in present times, we place our knives with the rounded edge pointing inward toward our plate when we set the table. We don't point our *weapon* toward any one.

How about the first fork? The fork came from the area now known as Turkey, although some think that it may have originated from Greece. It was big and beautiful, much too expensive for most people to use and it wasn't very useful. It was too large and had only two prongs—food slipped through.

Therefore, for many years, only the rich and famous of the day used it. It took many years for the fork to travel to people who would use it, besides royalty.

In the 1500s, the Italians made the fork useful for the masses and they used it for many years before Catherine de Médicis took it to France when she married Henry II.

In the 1600's an explorer presented the fork to the people of England. The English thought of it as something a feeble-minded person would use, because why would anyone use something like that when God gave us ten fingers?

TABLE BEHAVIOR

Basic manners are essential in everything we do and definitely a must at the table. The first and most important rule of the table is that we always want everyone to feel comfortable, because the essence of good manners is caring for those around you. This is the basic rule. If we keep this in mind, more than likely we will make the right decision.

So, we would always use all our manners like please, thank you, excuse me and please pass the… And, when someone asks for the salt, pass the pepper also. These, travel in pairs.

WHICH UTENSIL?

An easy rule to follow is to use the utensil that makes the most sense. Say that you are faced with a dish that has chunky food in a yummy sauce. You may want to use a fork because you want to stab the chunks of food items. However, if you want to taste the sauce, you may want to use your spoon. This is a personal decision and neither choice is incorrect. Just choose the utensil that makes the most sense for you to use at that time.

If the following course requires the utensil you just used and it has been removed, no problem. For this type of meal, you could just ask for another utensil or it will be brought out for you automatically.

WAIT UNTIL ALL ARE SERVED

Additionally, wait until all are served to begin eating. If we begin to eat before everyone is served, we appear greedy. This rule derives from a very old rule in which we would wait for the hostess to pick up her fork. This is tantamount to the dinner bell ringing. Additionally, one of our basic table-manners rules is that people are more important than the food. Thus, we wait.

ABOUT YOUR NAPKIN

Women, try not to leave lipstick marks on your glass by blotting your lips before the meal begins. Do this using a tissue, not your napkin. Speaking of napkin use, use your napkin to blot your mouth before drinking, as food and grease marks on the rim of a glass are unsightly.

If your napkin is a flimsy paper napkin, it isn't necessary to place it on your lap as you may get food on your clothes. When using one, you may place it on the table after blotting your mouth. Just try to conceal any food bits, so you don't make the other diners uncomfortable. Perhaps you could also place a clean napkin in your lap that will not be used so as to protect your clothes from spills.

NAPKIN RULES

- Placed the napkin on the left of the place setting or on the plate if the dinner is formal.
- Place the napkin in your lap after everyone has been seated.
- If you leave the table for a moment, place the napkin to the left of the plate or on the chair.
- Blot your mouth before taking a drink.
- Neatly place the napkin to the right of the plate when finished.

STRANGE FOODS

There are many types of food with which we may not be acquainted. In fact, in the United States, we didn't receive our first kiwi until the eighties. It seems as if we are faced with new foods every day now. So, if you are ever in doubt of what to do with a food or utensil during a meal, watch what the host does.

OBSCURE RULES

This may be an obscure rule, but we should cut and eat only one bite at a time. When we cut more than a few bites of food at one time, it appears as if we are overly eager to finish the meal. In addition, we wouldn't want those around us to feel as if we are anxious to leave the table.

Another obscure, slightly used rule these days is that children should wait until the adults are seated before sitting. This is a very old-fashioned rule that many do not observe. However, it may be observed during formal meals. Hence, be aware.

Do not blow on hot food. It seems as if everyone does this. So, why is this behavior incorrect? It is logical if you think about it. If you blow on your food, you could share more than conversation by accidentally blowing bits of food on other diners and sharing germs. You may also seem overly interested in speeding up your meal.

SENSITIVE ISSUES

Sometimes we can have something in our mouths that is very unpleasant such as gristle or a bone. The protocol for removing this unpleasantness from the mouth is to spit it out discretely onto the same utensil used to put it in our mouth and place it on our plate. Please try to be as discreet as possible.

There is no way to be discreet when we need to sneeze or cough. When the urge strikes, we sneeze and cough into our napkin pointing our head away from the table and follow it with, "Excuse me." However, if we must blow our nose or if we are coughing extensively, we excuse ourselves from the table—we never blow our nose into our napkin. This is simply respect for others at the table.

ELBOWS IN!

A great oldie but goodie rule is the one about our elbows. We all know this one: elbows should be close to our sides, not flapping about or placed on the table. However, did you know that we may place our elbows on the table in certain circumstances? Absolutely! The one exception is when you are having a conversation with a tablemate. If you place your utensils down on the plate, you may lean forward with an elbow on the table. This body language conveys that you are interested in what he or she is saying.

MOTHER RECOMMENDED RULES

Do you remember *your* mother telling you to chew with your mouth closed? Watching someone eat with his mouth open is disgusting. No one wants to view your half-eaten food as you slosh it around in your mouth. Therefore, we should chew with our mouths closed.

Another excellent *mother recommendation* – a rule you will be teaching -- is to take one bite at a time never overstuffing your mouth. If your face is distorted, you have too much in your mouth; and please, chew without talking. Food flying everywhere is nauseating.

BREAD AND BUTTER RULES

Finally, if using butter with bread, follow these steps. Using the butter knife, take a portion of butter and place it on your bread plate. Tear one piece of the bread or roll; spread the butter on the bread with your butter spreader, then take a bite.

- Your bread plate is on your left above your forks.
- Take one piece of bread at a time.
- Put butter on your plate with the butter knife or place knife.
- Tear one piece of bread and butter that piece.
- Eat one piece of bread at a time.

As important as it is to know what we *should* do at the table, we need to know what we definitely should *not* do. Here are some absolute do not (s).

DO NOT

- Hover over your food.
- Hold your utensils like shovels.
- Reach.
- Place a utensil on the table after it is used.
- Blow on hot food.
- Wear any type of hat at the table.
- Make rude noises or engage in bad habits at the table.
- Lick your fingers.
- Push food onto your fork using your fingers.

Always remember that all manners derive from the basic instinct to treat people kindly. Therefore, it follows, that we would want everyone at the table to feel comfortable.

SETTING THE TABLE

An informal place setting would have a salad fork on the far left of the plate (Americans usually eat salad for a first course) with the dinner fork next to it, closest to the plate. The napkin is placed to the left of the forks or in the center of the plate, if the dinner is formal. The plate is in the center of the place setting. If you are having soup, the bowl is usually placed on top of the plate. The knife and spoon(s) are placed on the right of the plate with the sharp edge of the knife pointed toward the plate.

Place glasses above the knife in descending order according to size. Many people enjoy wine with dinner; if this were the case, there would be a water glass above the knife and a wine glass, or two, to its right.

If a bread plate is used, it would be placed above the forks with the spreader across the top of the plate, rounded side of the knife pointed toward you.

While we could discuss formal place settings here, it is not necessary. Utensil placement and number is logical. With each course, you would use a different utensil; for example, if you will be serving a salad, a fish course and an entrée you would set three forks to the left of the plate to be used in the order in which you eat the courses.

HOLDING AND USING UTENSILS

Now that the table is set, it is time to be seated. Place napkins in laps after everyone is seated at the table. There are a few reasons for this. One reason is that it is customary for men to rise as ladies enter the dining room. Another is that you would not want to appear to be overly anxious to get to the meal--people are more important than the food.

With everyone seated at the table, napkins in laps and food on the plates, it is time to discuss proper utensil use. There are two methods of using our utensils. One is the Continental method, which is used in Europe (most people who use fork, knife and spoon use this method) and the other is our zigzag or American method. One has to wonder why there are two different methods. Well, here too there are two theories about how this came about.

THE AMERICAN METHOD

AMERICAN METHOD TRIVIA

The first theory about how the American Method began is boring but probably true. In the 1600s, we Americans were cut off from Europe by distance and culture. There was one account of a Governor Winthrop of the Massachusetts Bay Colony using a fork in our colonial America. The rest of us, however, had no forks because they were too expensive so we continued to use the blunted knives imported from Europe.

Because these were not easy to eat with, we began to use our spoon to steady food while cutting. We would then have to switch the spoon to the right hand to scoop up the bite of food.

The second, more sexy (yes, table manners can be sexy), theory draws us to the times leading up to the American Revolution. The theory postulates that because one could never know who was on which side of the conflict, the revolutionists devised a method of identifying each other. They would enter a pub or eating establishment and the person who placed his knife down and switched hands to eat their bite was a fellow revolutionary.

It really doesn't matter which theory is correct, but the second is much more exciting.

HOW TO USE THE AMERICAN METHOD

The first style I will describe is the American method, or the zigzag method, most commonly used here. Hold the handle of the fork in your left palm with your index finger along the back of the fork, tines facing down. While holding your food with the fork, hold the knife in the palm of your right hand (if you're right handed) with index finger guiding it as you cut one bite of food at a time. (Reverse this if left handed)

When finished cutting, place the knife on the edge of the plate, sharp edge toward you, and move the fork to your right, or dominant hand, to take the bite with tines up. While the fork is in your right hand, you may scoop or stab anything on your plate. To help guide food onto the fork, you may use your knife or a piece of bread as a *pusher*.

THE CONTINENTAL METHOD

HOW TO USE THE CONTINENTAL METHOD

The Continental or European style of holding and using utensils is very interesting and utilitarian.

While holding the utensils in the same manner as the American method, you cut the bite. Keep the fork in your left hand with fork tines down and take the bite by guiding the fork to your mouth—all the while with tines facing down. You may push food onto the back of the fork as well. You may keep the knife in your right hand awaiting the next cut or place it on the edge of the plate--sharp edge pointed toward you. (Reverse this if left handed)

If you would like to stab or scoop food, you may use the fork in either hand. However, it is *most* proper to scoop food with fork tines down and using the knife or bread as a pusher.

EATING SOUP

It doesn't matter which method you use for fork and knife. Soup is eaten the same manner.

While eating soup hold your *larger* spoon as you would a pencil. Scoop the soup away from you filling the bowl of the spoon no more than ¾ full. Bring the spoon to the lips and pour the liquid into your mouth. However, do not put the entire spoon into the mouth. Return the spoon to the bowl or the plate underneath. It is proper to tip the bowl to get the last of the soup, but never pick the bowl up to drink. And, never slurp.

BASIC TIPS

- Hold your *larger* spoon as a pencil to eat soup.
- Scoop the soup away from you.
- Never place a utensil on the table after it is used.
- Everyone should have food on his plate before starting to eat.

BODY LANGUAGE & TABLE CONVERSATION

BODY LANGUAGE

Body language is so very important in everything we do, because our body language speaks for us. It is an indication of how we feel about ourselves, those around us, and about our environment. So please, be attentive to the way you sit at the table.

So what is the proper body language at the table? We do not slouch, rock, or tip in your chair. Instead, we sit up straight, but relaxed and not stiff. Alternately, don't sit overly stiff so as to dribble food all over the front of us. We lean forward slightly from our *hips* when taking a bite—bringing the food to our mouth, not our mouth to our food.

Getting back to the subject of tipping and rocking in our chairs, I have a very good friend who is quite stout. Recently, he joined us for a nice brunch, and because he is quite large, he bent one of my chairs by merely tipping back. I was so embarrassed for him, but thankfully, he did not notice the chair. It would have ruined our enjoyable afternoon.

What kind of grooming would you imagine would be allowed at the table? Trick question! There is no grooming at the table, including picking your teeth, cleaning your nails, combing your hair and apply makeup at the table.

If there is something stuck in your teeth, excuse yourself to the restroom. Additionally even though some restaurants may provide toothpicks – at a counter by the door – (*I wish it wasn't so*) these are not for use at the table or for use in the presence of others. Using a toothpick has the same effect as flossing at the table.

Finally, our last reminder speaks to those whose heads are always so cold that wearing their hats to the table seem appropriate. Don't. Just please remember what your first grade teacher probably told you every day. Don't wear your hats indoors, *especially* at the table

RULES TO REMEMBER

- No hats at the table.
- Do not apply makeup, clean fingernails, or comb hair at the table.

TABLE CONVERSATION

Our basic instinct at the table is to share, so it follows that conversation is very important. Conversations should be pleasant, never argumentative and should include everyone equally. Humor is usually welcome; however, degrading jokes are not.

Keep the conversation light, talk about the day, current life events and friends. Discussions about your foot fungus are definitely off the menu.

This is also a great opportunity to introduce to children the rule of not interrupting others. We want a peaceful setting in which to enjoy the meal and the company of others.

The pace of consuming food slows as we share pleasant conversation, as if we are "Savoring the flavor." If you find that you tend to rush through your meal, perhaps savoring the flavor could be your new motto. Others should not feel obliged to rush through their meal to catch up with you. Be considerate, slow it down and enjoy the company and the meal you share.

Please

- No ethnic humor, disgusting topics, politics or religion.
- No discussions of bodily functions.

STYLES OF MEALS

FORMALITY MATTERS

There are three styles of meals, two of which are formal. One style of formal meals is courses brought out on platters and in bowls and served to the guests. The second is very formal. Food is plated in the kitchen and placed in front of each diner.

Informal dinners are often served family style, which means food is placed on the table in serving bowls and plates. Food is passed from the left to the right to avoid a traffic – or food – jam, and a disorganized mess. When eating family style, assist the person on your right by holding the bowl or plate after making sure the diner on your left has served himself. Please watch your serving size to make sure that there is enough food for everyone.

FAMILY STYLE MEALS

- Begin when the host begins.
- Serve yourself after the person on your left has served herself.
- Assist the person on your left and right with their serving.
- Pass the pepper with the salt.

FORMAL MEALS

Formal dinners may be plated in the kitchen and served to each diner. Alternately, servers may offer each diner servings from trays and bowls. In both cases, the meal will be served from the left, so lean slightly to assist the server.

If the meal is brought out on trays and bowls, you need to work a bit. With meat or anything served on a tray that cannot be stabbed, slide the serving spoon under the item while steadying it with the serving fork – *hopefully* – guiding it successfully to your plate. When served vegetables or any food that can be scooped, use the serving spoon to scoop an appropriate serving on to your plate. If there is a sauce or gravy, use the ladle or pour directly from the gravy boat (pitcher) onto meat, rice, or potatoes.

FORMAL MEAL RULES

- Enter the dining room when asked.
- Locate your place card and stand behind that chair until everyone has entered.
- A menu card may be on your plate or between diners.
- There will be salt and pepper for each diner or for every two.
- Finger bowls: dip fingers and dry on your napkin.

BEHAVIORS TO TEACH

- Remember to say please, thank you, and excuse me.
- Reinforce not interrupting others, because we share at the table.
- Remind children not to stuff their mouths.
- Cut one bite at a time and don't talk with mouths full.
- Wait until everyone is seated before placing the napkin in our laps and eating.
- Discussions should be pleasant, and everyone should be involved.

Dinnertime is the perfect opportunity to reinforce all of these behaviors along with the finer points.

Children should assist with setting the table, not just because they need to share in the responsibilities of the home, but also because they will learn utensil placement. They will learn where the napkin is placed and where we place glasses. Encouraging your child to help will benefit the entire family.

Most of all, your dinner hour should be a time in which you share your day and your child gets to know you and your values. As you model the behavior you wish for your child, he will learn very quickly and effortlessly. Enjoy your family; before you realize it, they will have families of their own.

CHAPTER SEVEN
DINING OUT

THE IMPORTANCE OF TABLE MANNERS WHILE DINING OUT

Always take proper table manners with you, even when visiting a fast food restaurant. While it's not necessary to cut a hamburger with a fork and a knife or place a flimsy paper napkin in our lap, we still eat with our mouths closed. We also use quieter tones because we know others are there to eat, not to listen to our loud voices.

Of course dining out is a perfect opportunity to display our table manners. Perhaps you could take your child to the restaurant of his choice after he masters the finer points. Once he knows to choose a utensil from the outside first and to place the napkin in his lap, he is well on his way.

Do you remember my story about the boy in the restaurant? Here is another similar story. Recently, my husband and I took my daughter and two-year-old grandson to a fast food restaurant because he *loves* fries. In contrast to my grandson's perfect behavior, a boy approximately eleven-years-old was playing at the table and in the aisle.

The exit was close to their table where Dad and another boy were seated. This young man went outside and made faces through the glass at the others seated at the table. *Very entertaining.* Worse yet, his feet were in a flowerbed. He showed no respect for the

owners of the restaurant, the patrons who were there to eat, or the property.

Were the boys in my stories the only ones responsible for their disrespectful behavior? No. The fathers were watching in both cases. Why did they allow this behavior? We are, after all, visitors to these properties. A restaurant is a place to eat and share a pleasant atmosphere; it does not matter if the property is a fine dining or fast food establishment.

Perhaps the problem with the fathers mentioned above lies in the fact that we all work so much. Many of us are away from home for long periods, so we don't have time to be with our children. Then, when we are out, we don't want to discipline them. After all, there is very little time we can share with our children.

Is this the correct approach? I don't think so. Children need to know their boundaries. They need to know that they cannot make up the rules as they travel through life. What kind of life will they lead if they believe that they can behave as they wish wherever they want?

Teaching respect for others and property is a parent's duty. Don't miss those teachable moments. When your child acts as these boys did, please pull them aside, discreetly, and remind him that he is a visitor. You will not ruin the event. You are trying to prepare your child for his future. Sometimes that means that you must get out of your chair and act. He will still love you.

I realize that this may be difficult to accomplish, because unfortunately the television constantly runs programs and commercials with 'cool' looking guys eating like (choose your noun). However, this is where you step in to act as the television editor. Help your child realize that these bits of mind candy are meant to sell something, not to promote a lifestyle. Sorry, but this is your job.

In order to do this difficult job, the following chapter offers a dining-out tutorial.

DINING OUT BASICS

When we visit a restaurant, any kind of restaurant, we are just visiting. We need to show respect for property, other diners and those who work there. Please treat the wait-staff with respect; they are people, not just fixtures.

A reservation at a restaurant is reservation for a specific time. Therefore, punctuality is paramount; it is not respectful to the proprietors if you waste their time by arriving late. If you have not made a reservation, please ask politely for inclusion. Pushy, elitist behavior or attitudes are rude and not acceptable behavior no matter how important this dinner may be. This is also something we don't want to teach our children.

Once you are seated and receive your menus, try to choose quickly. This does not mean you cannot talk to your companions only that the wait staff has others to serve. Ask about specials, including prices, and any ingredients of which you are unsure. It is much better to take the time to be sure what is in your meal before receiving it, rather than be disappointed and need to send it back.

If you are a guest, wait for the host to mention what he is ordering. He may want to order a bottle of wine and want to pair it with the food. Additionally, perhaps this meal is meant to be on the *light* side so you would not want to order too much. In any case, it is always best to order mid-priced choices. In addition, please thank the host for the invitation. (This is a great teachable moment for your child as well.)

If you are the host and you want your guest to know he may order anything, mention that there are wonderful first courses that he may wish to try. You may want to comment about the luscious desserts.

Additionally, remember that conversation is as important as the meal you share. So, as you converse, place your utensils on your plate in an upside-down V shape. Usually, the wait staff recognizes this as a rest in the meal. However, when you are finished with the meal, place your utensils parallel to each other on the right side of the plate. This is the sign for your wait staff to retrieve the setting.

GENTLE REMINDERS

- Stay in your seat; remind your child as well.
- No loud noises, only quiet tones.
- Act respectfully of other's spaces; be mindful of your coat, bags and no cellphones.
- Use proper table manner.
- Be on time for reservations.
- Model kind behavior toward staff.
- Wear appropriate clothing.
- Always think of others and how your actions will affect them.

CHAPTER EIGHT
FINGERS, FORK AND KNIFE

I REALLY NEED TO KNOW THIS!

In order to teach your child how to eat all foods, you will need know how yourself. So, follow along as we learn how to eat certain foods.

COMMON FINGER FOODS

- Artichoke
- Asparagus
- Bacon, if it is crisp
- Sandwiches
- Cookies
- Small fruit or berries with stems
- French fries and potato chips
- Hamburgers and hot dogs
- Corn on the cob
- Caviar

- Pickles
- Olives
- Tacos

HOW DO I EAT THESE?

Apples:

Quarter apples with a fruit knife or steak knife; the core is cut away from each piece and pieces are eaten with the fingers. If you choose to remove the skin, pare each piece separately.

Artichoke:

Eat artichokes with the fingers one leaf at a time. Dip leaves into the sauce provided. Eat the fleshy part of the leaf, scraping it off between your teeth. Place the leaf on the side of your plate. Remove the choke, the small leaves with sharp points, with your spoon and add to the eaten leaves. Cut the heart into sections using a fork and knife, and dip with the fork into the sauce to eat.

Asparagus:

At a formal dinner, use a fork and knife, cutting one bite at a time. Individual tongs may be used at a *very* formal dinner. In casual settings, asparagus is a finger food if firm and not in a sauce.

Bananas:

At a *formal meal*, peel the banana with fork and knife, eating one bite at a time. However, a whole banana would not be served at a formal meal. Thus, you would eat each smaller piece with a fork and knife. For informal meals, use your hands.

Barbecued Meats:

Barbeque is informal. Hot dogs, hamburgers, ribs and small chicken pieces are treated as finger food. To eat steak, fish, and large chicken pieces, use a fork and steak knife, cutting one bite at a time. Add sauce to your plate, if desired.

Berries:

In a formal setting, a strawberry fork may be used—just spear. If they have a stem, it is finger food. Ladle the sauce or cream onto your fruit plate before dipping.

Bread and Butter:

Break off a small piece of bread, place butter onto the bread plate using a butter knife. Use your knife to spread butter onto bread.

Caviar:

Caviar is finger food. Use the caviar spoon, usually small and round, and place a small amount on your plate or triangular toast that is usually served with caviar. If condiments are served, such as chopped onion, place a small amount on top of the caviar.

Cheese:

Spread soft cheeses such as Brie with the knife provided onto crackers or bread. With firmer cheeses, use the knife to slice a piece and place it onto your plate.

Cherry Tomatoes:

Cherry tomatoes are finger foods, unless it is served in a salad or other entrée. Break the skin in your mouth before chewing. If they are served in a salad or other dish, cut and eat using the fork.

Prick the skin to allow the juice to run first to avoid a messy juice explosion.

Chicken:

Never eat chicken with the fingers in a formal dining situation. In an informal setting, you can eat the smaller pieces with the fingers unless it is in a sauce. Larger pieces, such as chicken breasts must be cut using a place or steak knife.

Clams and Oysters:

While holding the shell in one hand and fork in the other, spear the clam, dip it in the sauce and eat it in one bite. You may suck the clam or oyster off the shell at an informal setting.

Condiments:

Place the condiments on to your plate before adding to a food item.

Corn on the Cob:

This is an informal food and is never served at a formal event. Eat with your fingers.

Crackers for Soup:

Place crackers for soup onto the bread plate. Break up into pieces and scatter into the soup.

Grapes:

Snap off a cluster, place on your plate and eat one at a time with fingers.

Lobster:

Pull the meat out with cocktail fork and dip it into melted butter or any sauce that is provided. Eat the tail meat by pulling out one piece at a time. If you pull out a particularly large piece, cut it with your dinner knife or fork before dipping.

Place the empty shell pieces onto a separate waste bowl or plate.

Melon:

At informal meals, melon is considered a finger food; however, it should be eaten with a fork and knife at other times.

Mussels:

Spear mussel, dip in sauce and eat it.

Oranges or Another Citrus:

In formal meals, cut off top and bottom, and slice off peel. Eat segments with fingers or fork and knife. For informal meals, peel with your hands.

Papaya:

Cut papaya in half; take out seeds with spoon, placing seeds on the side of plate. Eat with a fork or spoon.

Peas:

Scoop onto your fork or push using bread or your knife. Never guide with your finger.

Pizza:

Eat with a fork and knife unless the slices are firm.

Salad:

It is always best to use both a fork and knife.

Shish Kabob:

Hold the shish kabob in one hand and use the dinner fork to remove the pieces with the other. Place the stick on the side of the plate. Eat with a fork and knife.

Shrimp:

Small shrimp may be dipped into cocktail sauce using the cocktail fork. Eat large shrimp with fork and knife and place sauce on plate.

Snails/Escargot:

Pick up one at a time using tongs and remove with a cocktail fork—dip into butter.

Soups:

Eat clear soup with a small, round spoon, never filling more than 75% full. Eat from the side of the spoon, never placing the entire spoon into your mouth.

A cream soup is served with a medium round spoon, chunky soups with a large round spoon, and an oval spoon is used for all types of soup and some desserts.

A cup with handle may be picked up and drunk. Never pick up a bowl to drink the soup and never slurp. Place the spoon on the side of the plate when finished.

Spaghetti:

Never cut pasta with fork and knife. Use a fork and twirl until the strands are firmly wrapped around the fork. If there are strands dangling from the fork, take the bite allowing the strands to fall to the plate, use the fork to guide the strands.

Sushi:

Sushi may be eaten with the fingers or chopsticks.

CHAPTER NINE
THE WORKBOOK

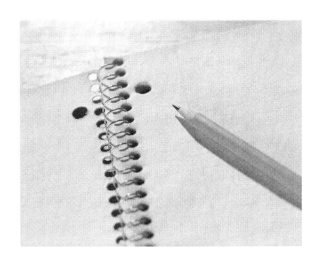

LET'S REVIEW

Chapter One

1. Create a teachable moment and describe what you taught your child.

   _____
   _____
   _____

Most any time you share with your child could be a teachable moment of active parenting. Make it fun by attempting to learn with your child.

2. How do you treat your significant other? What special things do you do to display respect for him/her? If there is no significant other, how do you teach your child respect for others?

   _____
   _____
   _____

3. What are your special moments with your child? How could you create more significant moments?

   _____
   _____
   _____

Suggestions:

- *Baking cookies/cake/treats together.*
- *Reading stories.*
- *Bird watching.*
- *Playing a game.*

4. What chores do you require of your children?

_____

_____

_____

Suggestions:

- *Feed and care the pets.*
- *Set the table.*
- *Wash the dishes.*

Chapter Two

1. Describe your child's body language. How will you help her/him to gain better body language?

_____

_____

_____

Your answer could be for you to display proper body language and discuss the importance often.

2. List three conversation starters.

_____
_____
_____

Suggestions:

- *Tell me about yourself.*
- *Follow up with the theme of an on-going conversation.*
- *Mention music playing in the background and ask the person's preferences.*

3. When is the last time your child wrote a "thank you" note/letter? Did you help her/him write one? To whom?

_____
_____
_____

Chapter Three

1. How do you teach your child how to respect property? How would you discipline your child if he/she was tossing items off a store shelf?

_____
_____
_____

It would be best to set behavior expectations before leaving the house. Make sure he/she understands by asking him/her to repeat expectations. Remind your child once of expected behavior if needed. If negative behavior continues, take the child home. Ensure your child knows that it was the behavior that was "bad" and not him/her.

2. Create an "dress-up" occasion. Describe the attire choice and the response of your child.

_____

_____

_____

Occasion Suggestions:

- *A play.*
- *Tea party—private or with guests.*
- *A special dinner.*

3. List three behavior rules for shared spaces.

_____

_____

_____

Suggestions:

- *Arrive on time for appointments*
- *Do not ride a skateboard at the mall.*
- *To be quiet, especially in waiting rooms.*

Chapter Four

1. How would you solve this problem? You are backing out of a parking spot when another car comes from around a corner and hits you. The driver emerges and is yelling about how this is all your fault, which, of course, it is not. How will you help your child learn how to deal with angry people, especially when they are wrong?

_____
_____
_____

It is best to keep your child in the car. Stay calm, lower your voice and reply that since you both do not agree on who is at fault, both should take pictures of the accident, exchange information and allow the insurance company to determine fault. If the person is behaving too aggressively and is abusive, the police should be called.

Chapter Five

1. How could you help your child learn to stay safe?

_____
_____
_____

Suggestions:

- *To keep all doors locked when home.*
- *Not to open doors for strangers when they knock.*
- *To have a house key when out of the house.*

Chapter Six

1. Why is it best to wait until all sit at the table before beginning to eat?

_____
_____
_____

It is best because it could appear as if you do not care about the other diners. One of the basic rules is that "People are more important than the food."

2. Name four table-manners rules you will teach your child. How will you teach them?

_____
_____
_____
_____

Suggestions:

- *Chew with your mouth closed*
- *Put your napkin in your lap after everyone has sat down.*
- *Sit up straight and do not hover over your food.*

- *Butter only one small piece of bread; not the entire piece.*

Chapter Seven

1. How are you helping your child understand that his/her behavior matters in restaurants? How are you preparing her/him before you arrive at the restaurant?

_____
_____
_____

Staying in his/her seat and using an indoor voice is a great start.

Most of what I have written in this book is review for you, I'm sure. Nevertheless, sometimes we are just too busy to consider exactly how we should teach our children manners. Act today. Watch for those teachable moments. Moreover, enjoy your family.

Good parenting.

YOUR AUTHOR

Your author, Rebecca Black, also known as The Polite One, recently retired from her company **Etiquette Now!** after a successful and rewarding 20+ years. As the owner and facilitator of her company, this retired elementary school teacher designed and presented custom etiquette workshops for the individual, corporate, governmental and educational client. Due to her extensive knowledge of the subject, she is also a well-respected author of etiquette books and lesson plans.

Considered an expert in the field, Rebecca answers etiquette questions (Q & A) and offers advice through her blogs: Got Etiquette Advice, Got Wedding Etiquette, and The Polite One's Insights.

Although for many years, Rebecca, focused her writing on etiquette issues, she is currently following her passion of writing fiction. A few of her most recent children's books also focus on the environment: *Save the Jellywonkers: Help Keep The Oceans Clean; Beware the Blackness, A Jellywonker Adventure;* and *The Tale of a Bear & Pony: A Yellowstone Adventure*

Please visit rebeccablackauthor.blogspot.com for more information about Rebecca's current news.

Connect with Us
https://www.facebook.com/ThePoliteOne

https://www.facebook.com/rebeccablackauthor/

Visit Us
Rebecca Black Author

Etiquette Now! Insights

Got Etiquette Advice

Got Wedding Etiquette

Living Well & Enjoying Life—Rebecca Style

The Polite One's Insights

The Polite Traveler

https://www.amazon.com/author/rebecca_black

Published Fiction Books by Rebecca Black
The Tale of a Bear & Pony; A Yellowstone Adventure

Save The Jellywonkers! -- Help Keep Our Oceans Clean

Beware the Blackness! A Jellywonker Adventure

Sapphire and the Atlantians

War in Atlantis

The Return of the Tui Suri

Published Etiquette Books by Rebecca Black

Dining Etiquette: Essential Guide for Table Manners, Business Meals, Sushi, Wine and Tea Etiquette

Dress for All Occasions—The Basics, Attire Must-Haves, Dress Code Definitions & FAQs

Entertaining Skills 101

Etiquette for The Socially Savvy Adult: Life Skills for All Situations

Etiquette for the Socially Savvy Teen: Life Skills for All Situations

Golf Etiquette: Civility on the Course

How to Tea: British Tea Times

How to Teach Your Children Manners: Essential Life Skills Your Child Needs to Know!

International Business Travel Etiquette: Seal the Deal by Understanding Proper Protocol

Navigating Important Events Without Appearing Clueless: Common sense advice, historical reflection and gift-giving savvy

Reach Your Potential: A guide to help you achieve your goals, be happier, and find your path

Societal Rage: Problem solving for our increasingly violent world

Sushi Etiquette: The guide for those who wish to eat sushi properly and avoid insulting the chef

Train the Trainer Guide: The essential guide for those who wish to present workshops and classes for adults

Wedding & Reception Planning: The Etiquette Guide for Planning the Perfect Wedding

Wine Etiquette--From holding the glass to ordering a bottle of wine in a restaurant and everything in-between

Workplace Etiquette: How to Create a Civil Workplace

Published Lesson Plans

Business Meal Etiquette

Career Fair Etiquette

Entertaining Skills 101: Lesson Plans for Those Who Wish to Present Workshops

Etiquette for the Socially Savvy Teen

Golf Etiquette

Growing Up Socially Savvy

How to Become a Socially Savvy Lady

How to Tea; British Tea Times

How to Teach Your Children Manners

Just for Teens, Skills for the Socially Savvy

Manners for Children

Organizational Skills

Prom Etiquette

Proper Business Attire

Skills for the Socially Savvy and Well-Dressed Teen

Skills for the Socially Savvy and Well-Organized Teen

Table Manners

Train the Trainer

Wine Etiquette

Workplace Etiquette

Wedding Lesson Plans

Lessons for the Newly Engaged

Wedding Planning

Wedding Reception Planning

Please visit https://www.amazon.com/author/rebecca_black for information about collecting more etiquette books.